It's Just Nature!

Fascinating Encounters With Animals

Table of contents

Introduction

Can I bring you into my nature world? You would not believe some of the things I've seen, from the bank fishing or walking to one of my favorite fishing spots. I have been involved in some of these myself, and in my 58 years of fishing, I have seen a few.

I want to try to get you out there around the rivers and lakes. Even if you do not fish, there is much in nature to see. My guess is that you might see something taking place in nature that you will not see on TV's nature channels.

Iowans and those who have lived in Iowa who may read this book, I want you to keep in mind that there are some nice walking trails around the rivers and lakes here in Iowa. I can think of a few places that come to mind that are in my area; places like Cedar Lake, Lake MacBride, and Palisades-Kepler State Park.

I hope you have some walking trails around the rivers and lakes in the area you live in. Don't wait, get out there, and get to walking and looking! You will never know what you might see, and the walk will be refreshing and good for you.

Chapter 1. Nature At Its Best!

We decided to go fishing one day – my uncle, myself, and two of my cousins. It was a nice day to fish. I always thought that it was a nice day to fish. Uncle decided to take us to a place called Big Sandy Creek. One of the main rivers in Tennessee fed this creek. I was about 10 years old then and didn't pay much attention to my surroundings. I was much too focused on where I was going to catch fish. When we got there, I found a good place to start fishing, but before I threw my bait in the water, I happened to look across to the other side of the creek and saw this big snake near the bank, heading toward a tree. This tree was in the water, at least most its tree roots were.

Most places on the Tennessee waters, you had to watch out for poisonous snakes. I watched that snake move toward those tree roots. I happened to look up into that tree and saw this kingfisher bird perched on a limb, and all at once, it was diving into the water, close to that big snake. What a catch that bird made. It had a fish in its beak and on its way out of the water, I thought for sure that bird was going to be that snake's breakfast with how long it took to get out of the water, but that big snake barely moved from those roots. I do not think that bird even saw the snake. That was neat to watch.

Chapter 2. That Woke Me Up!

Three days later, my uncle and I decided to go back to Big Sandy Creek where I had seen the kingfisher bird earlier. We had caught some fish there that day, so he and I decided to go back. We got there about 7:30 a.m. and I decided to fish on the medium high bank down the river, a little ways from my uncle. I chose this spot because there was a tree that fell in the water from alongside the bank. The water had washed some of the bank away from where the tree had pulled away from it, and all you could see was the roots.

The sun was shining and I baited up. As soon as my bobber hit the water alongside that tree limb, it went down. I had a crappie on my line; this happened about three times, and on the fourth time, when I was bringing in my fish and getting ready to lift that fish up, as I had did before, out of nowhere, this snake that I did not see and did not even know was down there around those tree roots, took a strike at my fish that I was pulling up. That nearly scared me to death; I almost dropped my pole and fish in the water as I jumped back. That snake had been there all the time in the shaded area of the tree roots, and when the sun was finally shinning on the snake, that got the snake moving.

4

That snake did not see me on the bank above it; it only saw that fish I was pulling up and it looked like something to eat, but it sure scared me good. I went and found a stick long enough to scare it away from my good fishing spot. That snake got very mad at me as I was trying to get it to move. It struck at that stick I had in my hand at least about three or four times before I got it to leave. Once it left, I did catch a few more fish before we went home.

Chapter 3. Too Close For My Comfort!

My family and I were on our way back to Tennessee; school had been out for about a month. I just knew fishing would be good when I got there. I had a feeling my uncle and aunts were already catching many fish because we were catching fish here in Iowa, and the weather in Tennessee is about 10 to 15 degrees warmer.

When we got there, my uncle and I decided we would go fishing if it were not raining, so we went that Monday morning. We headed to one of the Tennessee backwater areas, right off the Tennessee River. I was about 12 years old and a fair fisherman. When we got to the spot where we were going to fish, I got out of the truck and noticed there was a path and a sign down at the far end of the river, from where I was standing. That path looked like it would get you to the other side. My uncle told me if I were going to fish down at that end, I should be careful. Uncle said someone late summer last year got bitten by a snake down there, said he got off the path near the tree limbs in the water, and the high grassy bank near the water.

I decided to go that way and see what the sign said; the sign said beware of poisonous snakes. When I looked past that sign to the end, I could understand why there was a sign there. I could see high grass, logs, tree branches, and a lot of stuff bunched up at the edge of the bank near the water. I stood there and looked it over for a while, and now and then, you could see a big snake swimming around there. I could see the path swung way around that area, but I still was not going around there. I got within about 40 or 50 feet of the area, and there was a tree branch laying about 15 feet out in the water, so I stopped to fish right there because it was a clean spot and I could see all around me. I started to get my reel ready to cast out alongside of that tree branch and I noticed there was a fish at the end of that tree branch; it looked like a catfish that was hooked and could not get away. I could see the line was all snagged up; that catfish looked to be hooked really well, and it was moving slow, but now and then, it would have a little burst of energy and struggle a little harder.

As I stood there watching this catfish, 15 feet out in the water from where I was standing, I saw this big snake open its mouth and tear that catfish right off that snag. That scared me so bad; I dropped my pole, left my bait, and started running.

That was just too close to me. I waited for a while before I went back, got my fishing pole and equipment, and decided not to ever go near that area or fishing spot again. My uncle saw me running toward him and asked me what happened, and I told him.

Chapter 4. I Have Never Seen Anything Like This!

My family and I went to Tennessee during Summer Break, when I went to school; school got out the Friday before Memorial Day. We went down early that year for a Bryant family reunion. I could hardly wait to get there. Once again, my uncle and I were going to go fishing, but this time, my mom and two of my aunts wanted to go with us. So on a Monday, my uncle decided to go back to the place where he and I fished the last time I was with him the year before. We went to the Tennessee backwater area where that poisonous snake sign was, and where I had the big scare, but only this time, we fished at the opposite end. We got out of the truck and picked a good fishing spot – fishing was starting good that day.

When I got out of the truck, I thought I heard a noise that sounded like a big truck, but I couldn't see anything. A little later that morning, it sounded like that truck noise was getting even closer. When I looked down the riverbank again, I could see this big truck coming around the bend our way, slowly.

I stopped fishing and watched for a while. I could see that this truck had two big arms on it and it was pulling a trailer that looked as if it had long wood poles on it. I watched it stop as four big men got out of it; two of the big men had long sticks in their hands.

They went to the water edge with these sticks, and it looked to me like they were checking the water depth from the bank. I decided to put my fishing pole down and walk down a little closer to see what they were doing.

The men saw me coming that way, so they stopped me about 50 feet from where they were working and told me I could not come any closer. I stood there and watched those two big arms on that truck pick up one of those telephone poles off that trailer straight as an arrow. I watched as two of the men stepped into the water, waist deep with their chest waders on, heavy-duty rubber gloves on, and their harness secured to the truck. I watched as the two men in the water helped steady the pole as the big arms held it and pounded it at the same time, deep into the riverbank's edge. The other two men on the bank, with their knee boots and heavy-duty gloves on, helped steady the pole too. They worked at this for about an hour or two.

When they came out of the water, I did not believe what I saw as the two men on the bank helped them out. I had gotten a little closer to the men now that they were getting out of the water and I had a good view. One of the men had two snakes stuck to his chest wader and the other man had just one. The snakes were wiggling and trying to get loose; that looked eerie to me.

The two men on the bank ran to the truck and got a big butcher knife. I watched as they cut those snake bodies off right to their head and then watched them pry their heads off carefully with a smaller knife they had gotten from the truck. They kept those big rubber gloves on, so as not to be bit as they carefully pried off those snakeheads.

I was close enough to ask those men how it felt to step into the water, knowing there might be poisonous snakes in that area. They told me that it was a good paying job working for the Electrical Company, laying telephone poles, and you had to get used to the hit of the snakes in the water because it was just part of the job. They told me all four of them took turns getting in and out of the water except the truck driver operator; he just smiles. I said goodbye to them as I walked back to my fishing spot. What a sight.

Chapter 5. A Battle To Remember!

Dad had retired so he and Mom moved to Atwood, Tennessee; a small town where they had family. My dad had two brothers and my mom had four sisters, all who lived there.

My brother and I decided to go down to visit them. The year before that, my brother and brother-in-law had moved my dad and mom to Tennessee, where they had bought a place.

My brother and I took off around the first of May to go check on them. I would not be able to fish with my uncle anymore; he had passed away and I sure was missing him every time I would go to Tennessee. I knew when I got there; my dad and mom would want to go fishing. My mom and I fished together in Cedar Rapids, Iowa, and my dad too if he was not working.

Dad and Mom had only been in Tennessee for about a year or so, so I asked them if they had found any good places to fish yet. They told me about some of the old fishing spots that I had fished as a young boy, but they also told me that one of my mom's sisters (my aunt) showed them a new place to fish. Dad said the only thing he did not like about this place was that you could not shoot a gun there because it was a Tennessee backwater duck refuge.

Dad and Mom decided we would go to a backwater duck refuge the next day, which was a Tuesday. Mom said it was about an hour or so away from the house, but they had been catching some nice fish there every time they went.

When I got out of the car, the place did not look too bad for fishing; we got there at about 7:30 a.m. After stopping at the bait shop, Mom told me to be careful walking any of the banks because of snakes; you could not shoot them here.

I noticed most of the banks were high except for a few places. Mom was right; seemed like everywhere you looked, you would see a snake. Dad and Mom were fishing on an old wooden handicap bridge that was over a waterway that flowed under it. I decided to walk down a utility roadway path that looked clean. I found a good-looking fishing spot along the bank where there was a tree limb in the water. I was only using jigs now and getting good at it. I started to catch some big bluegills around that limb. I happened to look across at the bank on the other side, and something got my attention in the stickweeds along the bank. I couldn't believe what I was seeing. I saw a big snake with its mouth around

13

the head of a catfish; that catfish had to be a least 7lb or more in size. Most of the big snake's body was on the bank as it was trying to pull that catfish out of the water onto the bank, but that catfish was big enough to pull back. What a battle this was; as the big snake would pull, the catfish would go into a roll, and then they would rest for a minute or so. I watched this battle for about a half an hour or longer in amazement. I did not know what was going to happen to that catfish, but I thought it had a good chance to get away. I could see that the big snake could not get its mouth past the side fins of that catfish, and so I did not think that the snake had enough venom in the catfish to kill it. Those side fins around the head of a catfish are very sharp and painful if you encounter them. They battled for a little while longer, and then the big snake finally let go. The catfish swam away very slowly as the big snake rested on the bank. WOW.

Chapter 6. I Made A Friend!

I was on my way fishing that day, it was a nice, partly cloudy morning and the temperature was about 58 degrees. I got to the lake about 5 a.m. and I knew that the temperature was going to get to about 80 degrees around noontime. It was a nice, fresh morning with a slight breeze hitting my face, coming out from the southeast.

What a day to be down at Lake MacBride fishing. Fishing was good that morning. I could pick and choose what I wanted to put in my bucket. The crappies were a nice size and I had about 12 that I had kept so far. I was planning on leaving about 11.

It must have been around 9:30 a.m. or so when I noticed down the bank a small animal making it way down toward me, and it did not look like it was afraid. I was a little afraid myself because it kept on coming toward me; I was ready to fight it off, if it was getting ready to do something.

It was a mink, and that mink got within about 6 feet of me before it stopped and checked my bucket with fish in it. The mink could not get in my bucket because I always had a lid on it, with a hole big enough to put fish in! I watched that mink as it circled my bucket, all the while stopping to look at me. I began to talk to it mink softly, as though it was a pet of mine. I tried to catch a fish to give to it, and I did; a small crappie about 3 or 4 inches long. I threw the fish on the bank within about three feet from me, the mink picked it up, looked at me and took off. Nothing like this had ever happened to me before while I was fishing.

Whenever I went to Lake MacBride and fished that spot where I had seen that mink, it would come to where I was fishing, seemed like out of nowhere. I would talk to it softly as I did before, that mink would circle my bucket, look at me and stay there until I would give him a fish. This went on for about 2 years or so, then one day that mink did not show up any more. I had lost my animal friend somehow! That was neat while it lasted!

Chapter 7. You Will Not Believe This!

I was on my way fishing that spring morning, what a beautiful sunrise it was, I got to the lake about 6 a.m., got out of my jeep, put on my hip boots, and got the rest of my fishing equipment together. I headed to the spillway. The spillway is where Lake MacBride's overflow spills right into the Iowa River.

As I was walking down to the spillway, I heard a duck quacking on the lake in MacBride. It was a mallard hen duck with three ducklings swimming close behind her. I was not in a big hurry that morning, I was just glad to be out there, so I stopped and watched, and I listened as the hen was quacking and swimming with her ducklings while I was enjoying the beautiful morning.

They were about 30 feet from the shoreline. As I was watching, all at once, I saw this big mouth open and take one of the ducklings! Man-o-man, that was unreal!

I watched that hen quack and quack, repeatedly. She was going around in circles looking for her lost duckling, as the other two ducklings were so close to her that it looked like they were riding on top of her. The hen finally settled down after about 15 minutes or so. She and her remaining two ducklings swam over to the bank a little distance away and got out of the water. I watched as the hen looked back into the water, quacking, looking as she was waiting for her lost duckling to come. That was a sad moment.

Chapter 8. Run For Your Life!

It was an early fall morning, around October 1. I decided to see if I could catch some of those big fall crappies that had been a little slow that spring. One of my favorite spots to fish for big crappies in the fall was at the spillway on the Iowa River Side, but I decided that morning to fish on Lake MacBride side, right next to the cliff, just before you got to the spillway on the Iowa River side.

The water from Lake MacBride was not spilling over to the Iowa River as it usually does in the fall; the water that spring and summer had been low. The state of Iowa had gotten very little rainfall all year long.

It must have been about 7:00 a.m. when I got to Lake MacBride. I walked toward the cliff and when I got there, I walked around the cliff, right to the spillway flat on the Lake MacBride side. This was an area on Lake MacBride that when the water was low, it was one of the deepest places that had big rocks, and tree limbs submerged so that you could not see, but you could feel as you were fishing it.

I stopped at the right spot that morning because I was doing pretty well. I had about seven nice crappies and a walleye about 21 inches long. I looked at my watch because the fishing had started to slow down a little; it must have been about 9:30 a.m., and I was going to leave about 11:30 a.m.

I heard this noise like something was running right above me in the wood adjacent to where I was standing. Lake MacBride has a few somewhat high cliffs along its water line. As I stopped fishing to listen, it sounded like something was being chased. The running sound got closer, closer, and closer, and then all of a sudden, this deer came running full speed, and jumped of the cliff adjacent to me as I watched from the spillway flat where I was standing.

The heights that deer jumped from must have been about 15 feet or more. What a sound and splash it made! That deer hit the water hard and must have stayed under water for about 10 seconds or more. The way it hit the water, I did not think it was ever going to come up. The deer finally came up, swam fast as it could across the lake, got out of the water, did not even shake itself off, and ran up the bank into the woods out of sight.

I never did see what was chasing that deer – it must have stopped just before the deer jumped off the cliff – and whatever it was really had that deer on the run.

Chapter 9. The Wind Was Blowing In The Right Direction!

I thought I would check this spot out. I found myself walking through a weedy, wooded area on the Iowa River that nice spring morning. As I got through it, there was a nice, clear area of bank to fish. I began walking and jigging this long clearing of bank. I was a short distance away from that weedy, wooded area I came from, and I caught my first fish, a nice crappie.

It was about 10:30 a.m. and fishing was a little slow. In my bucket, I had three crappies and two white bass. I had walked about two miles or so, and decided it was time to head back. I got within about 40 feet of where I came out of the weedy, wooded area and I get a hit, my fourth crappie as I landed it. I turned to put that crappie in my bucket, and as I turn back to start fishing again, to my surprise, right there at the edge of the weedy, wooded area where I had came from earlier was a mother coon and two of her babies.

This sow coon was big, sitting on her haunches she was about 3 feet tall, and not only that but she was looking dead at me with her head in the air sniffing, I am sure, while her babies played at the water's edge.

If you could have asked me at that moment what was going on in my mind, I would have told you that I was one scared man, looking for some kind of protection, because I did not know what was going to happen.

The wind was blowing in the right direction that morning and she could not smell me, as her and the babies cleared the weedy, wooded area near the water. I felt I was close enough to them to be in harm's way; any mother with babies is dangerous. I began to move out of the danger zone slowly. As I watched her, she watched me as I moved away.

Finally, this sow coon stopped watching me and got off her haunches. I watched as she was teaching her babies how to look for food, turning over rocks, catching crayfish, and whatever else she could find, while the babies played most of the time. It was fun watching the babies play while she hunted for food. They must have stayed for about an hour or so, and then she and the babies waddled back into the weedy, wooded area.

Chapter 10. It's Time To Eat!

I decided to take a vacation day to go fishing; I had about five weeks to use up. I asked for a vacation day for a Thursday and I got it. The weatherman said it was going to be partly cloudy that day and the temperature was going to be in the low 80. It was supposed to rain Monday and Tuesday of that week, according to the weatherman's five-day forecast; he was right this time, it did rain those two days. I was glad I decided to go on Thursday.

I got to the lake about 6 a.m. that morning, heading to the spillway on the Iowa River side. I fished a couple of spots until about 10 a.m. The water was a little dirty and coming up. I fished about 4 hours and only caught 8 fish. I had 5 white bass and 3 crappies in my bucket. I decided it was time to go; it had slowed down to nothing, and I should have left a half-an-hour or so earlier.

I started to head to my jeep for home, and decided to fish Lake MacBride for an hour or so before I left. I started walking around the trail to one of my favorite fishing spots.

As I was enjoying the walk, I heard all of this loud squalling. I looked up and saw these black birds in the trees; some were circling and diving down at something. I didn't know what was going on. I was getting close to my favorite fishing spot and all that noise and commotion was loud, and so I decided to slow down and become much more alert.

I have noticed at times that black birds have a way of warning if there is danger around. I found out what that noise and commotion was all about as I came around the bend. I watched as they squalled and dived. There in the woods, about 200 feet from the walking trail, was a beautiful red fox with a duck in its mouth.

The black birds had that fox so busy stopping and watching them that he didn't even see me. I watched that fox for about five minutes or so, trying to slip away for those noisy black birds. Finally, the black birds quieted down and the fox slipped out of sight with its prey in its mouth. What a great picture.

Chapter 11. Breakfast Time!

I decided to go fishing that morning; I headed to the spillway on the Iowa River side, down at Lake MacBride. What a beautiful 68-degree late spring morning. I got there about 6:30 a.m. and there was a slight breeze hitting me in the face as I got out of my jeep. I started walking toward the spillway, making sure I didn't forget anything, as I always get a little excited when I'm on my way fishing, no matter how many times I go!

I was almost there at the spillway, and as I was approaching the place I wanted to fish, there below me was a big black bird (raven), standing on a rock, and right below it, standing in the water, was a stork. I slowed my walk down to a stop, so as not to scare the two birds away, and with the water coming over the spillway into the Iowa River, they didn't hear me coming.

I had a great view, and I wanted to see what was going on. I watched as that raven acted as though it was a cheerleader for that stork. I watched that raven walk back and forth on that rock, squawking every now and then, moving its head up and down, as that stork fished at the water's edge, catching a fish every so often. I stood there for about 20 minutes or so, watching in amusement as that raven cheered that stork on. That was what it looked to me like that raven was doing, but I don't really think so. That stork did some pretty good fishing. It would miss a few but it didn't give up. While I was watching, that stork caught about three fish. I guess it finally got its belly full and flew off, and that raven was right on its tail. You just had to be there to see this take place, pretty funny.

Chapter 12. Follow The Leader!

It was an early fall morning in October; I was on my way to the Roller dam on the Cedar River. Two days before that, I had caught three nice walleyes and one big white bass, about 18 inches long. I got down to the river about 8:00 a.m. and the temperature was a little chilly; it was about 45 degrees.

The fishing was a little slow that day. It was going on about 9:30 a.m. and I only had one walleye about 20 inches long, and a white bass about 15 inches long, and I knew I had to leave about 11.

When I got to the river, I had noticed that there were only a few fishermen there. When I looked across the river on the north side, I saw only two guys fishing off the steel wall, and when I looked up toward the roller dam, I could only see one guy up there.

I thought maybe because the water was coming up a little this time of the year that it slowed the fishing down some, and the fishermen too. As I looked down the riverbank on the north side of the river below me, something caught my eye. I watched as a deer came out of the woods, down to the bank at the water's edge. As I kept watching that deer, six more came down. I thought that maybe they just came down for a drink of water.

I knew the water was coming up slow, but that also meant that the water currents were still strong. I watched them mill around the river bank for about five minutes or so, looking across the river every now and then. It looked like they were trying to make up their minds if they were going across or not. Just like that, one jumped in and started to swim across the river, and it took about five seconds for the next one to jump in, and then it became a chain reaction; one after another, until they all were in the water, swimming across the river.

I stood there as I had stopped fishing when I saw the first deer come down out of the wood to the water's edge. I watched all of them make it to the other side, and it looked like they were struggling to get there. The current had pushed them down the river a little ways but they made it out of the water, shook themselves off, stood there for a few minutes, and then took off into the woods. I had never seen that many deer at one time swim across a river like that before. That was really neat to watch!

Chapter 13. They Are Really Pretty!

It was a beautiful late fall morning and I had the day off, so I decided to go to one of my favorite fishing spots. I headed down to Lake MacBride.

I got out of my jeep, got my fishing equipment together and started heading toward the spillway on the Iowa River side. As I'm walking, I look across the river on the west side and I see all of this white moving very slowly in the water. It looked to be about a thousand birds packed together over there, swimming very slowly, all bunched up. I watched for about a minute or so, then right above where they were in the water, right off the shoreline, I could see something coming toward them. I heard barking! Then I saw them take flight all of a sudden; what an awesome sight.

The distance I was watching those birds from had me thinking they might be snow geese, but they looked a little big, even from where I was standing, and when they took flight, they were slow and graceful.

These birds circled and started to head the way I was going. They landed pretty close to where I was going to fish. They were snow pelicans, and they were beautiful. I had never seen this many birds before in the wild.

I stood there and watched those snow pelicans as they moved very slowly back and forth, feeding. I watched as they held their big mouths open in the water, like a shovel scooping up sand. I could see them scooping up bait fish, which looked to me like were shad. It was a sight to see so many of them. They stayed around where I was fishing all that morning. They caught fish and I didn't do so bad myself. What a beautiful sight to see!

Chapter 14. Things That Made My Mouth Drop!

I have been blessed as a fisherman to see some things happening while fishing, or on my way fishing, that made my mouth drop. In this chapter, I would like to share some of these moments with you that don't have a long storyline behind them. I was just blessed to be in the right place and at the right time to see it happen.

Story 1. I was fishing at Lake MacBride that morning and I was really enjoying the day. I was fishing in a real good spot and I was catching a few. Right in front of me was a moth, hovering right over the water. A fish all of a sudden came out of the water, about two inches or more, and grabbed that moth in mid air; awesome! It was a bluegill!

Story 2. It was an early fall morning and I decided to go fishing at Lake MacBride. I got there, got out of the jeep and I felt the wind hitting my face, not strong mind you; it was probably only blowing about five miles an hour or so.

I began looking at the lake to see if the water was very choppy, but what I saw was amazing. I could see school, and a school of bait fish everywhere being chased all over the lake, but what was so neat about it was that you could actually see some of the fish come out of water after the bait fish. It was pretty exciting; you had to be there to see the action! I watched this go on for about 15 or 20 minutes before I started to fish myself.

Story 3. It was about dusk on a late October day. I made it down to MacBride about 4 p.m., right after work. It must have been about 5:30 p.m. or so, and I had about 6 nice crappies and 2 walleyes, about 18 to 20 inches give or take.

The sun was setting and it was getting a little chilly, and it was still light enough on the fishing bank that you could see. I decided it was time to go, and I was getting a little tired because I had worked 10 hours that day. I was headed to my jeep and I got within about 30 feet from where I was parked. I stopped dead in my tracks! Coming out of the woods, 10 feet in front of my jeep, was one of the biggest bucks I ever saw. I watched him raise his massive head in the air, looking at me, moving his head back and forth, trying to catch my scent.

That big buck seemed like it was there forever, inching toward me, moving that massive head back and forth, pawing, and then it would stop to look and see if I would move. I didn't move a muscle at the time, but I knew I had to do something. I decided to drop my fishing bucket, yell, clap my hands, and jump up and down all at the same time. It worked; that big buck took off, running back to the woods. That was a close call!

Story 4. It was a nice, early summer day, and I decided to fish on the Iowa River, over by the broken bridge. The fishing that day was a little slow for me. I could not find the crappies, and the only fish I was catching that day was largemouth bass that were about 10 to 14 inches long. It was fun catching those largemouth bass, but that was not what I was looking for.

I was standing there fishing and I had been noticing minnow being chased right there in front of me. I watched as a minnow came out of the water right on the bank, being chased by a bass that ended up on the bank too. I watched as they both struggled to get back into the water; what a chase that was! That poor bass didn't even get its meal as they both made it back to the water safely.

Chapter 15. Let's Talk Turkey!

I was on my way to Lake MacBride on an early spring day in April to fish one of my favorite spots. I got inside the park, passed by the rangers house, turned right at the stop sign, and took another quick right on the gravel road that goes around behind the camp grounds that's in the park.

This gravel road is now a black top road that goes around to the Iowa River and as Lake MacBride fishing station as well. Anyway, as I was topping the hill, right around the corner, right in the middle of the road, and right along side of the road, were about 30 turkeys or more. They made me come to a complete stop because they would not get out of the roadway, and I did not even honk my horn.

I got close enough to those turkeys to run them over, because they were not even afraid. I stopped my truck right in front of them and turned it off because it looked like I was going to be there for a while. There were a lot of big turkeys in that group as I watched them eat and pick up small pieces of gravel on their way across the road.

The big Tom turkeys must have been the lookouts, because they kept an eye on me, and even came closer to my truck window from the road to check me out, as they moved very slowly. They must have taken about 15 minutes or longer crossing that gravel road. It was pretty neat to watch them. I had never in my life seen this many wild turkeys together at one time, and up close to them. They were ugly birds up close but yet a beautiful sight to see. I watched as they slowly crossed the gravel road, disappearing into the woods on the other side. That was really a showstopper, and made my day!

Chapter 16. The Rat Pack!

It was after work on a Thursday, about 4:00 p.m., and I decided to go fishing down at the Cedar Slough River; that's what it was called in my day, growing up. Now the name has been changed to Cedar Lake, and it's a great place to eat, bike, walk, and fish.

That day at the Slough, I wanted to fish on the side of the river where the railroad tracks were, because I had never fished on that side before. It looked like there were some nice, clean fishing spots over there, so I headed that way.

I made sure I had my fresh chicken livers that I just got at the store on my way over, my fishing equipment, and my flashlight, because I was planning on fishing a little bit after dark, and there were no pole lights on that side of the river near the rail road tracks.

I found a nice, clean spot to fish, but behind me was some weed, about 15 feet away, and it was near the railroad tracks also.

It was going on about 6:00 p.m. and I was starting to catch a few catfish. I was having fun keeping some and putting some back.

Now it was starting to get dark, but I could still see my truck, because I had parked it under a pole light down at the far end, which was about 300 feet away.

I started to hear some movement noise right behind me in the weeds, right next to the railroad tracks; it sounded like something was coming toward me in those weeds. It was a very uneasy feeling, because I had not heard or seen any movement or noises in the daylight when I was fishing in this spot, and so I decided to turn my flashlight on to see what was making that movement noise. I'm thinking to myself maybe it's a raccoon or a possum, and so I picked up a handful of loose rocks and sticks that were around me, yelled, and threw them into the weed to try and scare whatever it was away.

When I threw the rocks and sticks the first time into the weeds and shone my flashlight in there, the movement noise stopped for about a few seconds or so, and then it started back again when the light was off.

I shone my flashlight again and spotted what was in those weeds, making that movement noise coming toward me. They were rats, and not very small ones at that. I guess they must have smelled that fresh chicken liver, and waited until dark to check it out. I believe they were ready to eat and I was in their way, and nothing was going to stop them. I kept my flashlight on until I got my tackle box, fishing pole, and fishing bucket, making as much noise as I could. When I got things together, I took off as fast as I could toward my truck, leaving those fresh chicken livers behind, hoping those rats were not following me. That was a real night scare, and I never did that again.

Chapter 17. No Family Around!

I wanted to go fishing at an old place that I had not been for a while, so I decided to go under the Iowa River bridge, which is 1380 north/south. I was going to fish on the south side of the river under the bridge. I got down there, got out of my jeep, nobody else around, got my fishing equipment together and looked around a little before I headed to my fishing spot. I got about 15 steps from my jeep, and out of nowhere, right from the woods, this gray fox puppy came toward me.

I became a little afraid at what I thought might come next, I did not know what to expect. I picked up a stick that was nearby just in case I had to fight off that gray fox pup's mother, because that fox pup kept coming toward me.

I started watching the patch of woods where that gray fox pup came from very intensely to see if the mother fox was coming. Thank God the mother never showed up; what a relief.

The fox pup stop about five feet in front of me as though it was lost, sniffing, and it was looking me over to figure out what I was. Then it began to jump around like it wanted to play. I stuck the stick out that I had in my hand, and the fox pup grabbed it and we played tug-a-war for a little bit.

Then I decided to drop the stick because the gray fox pup was not a threat to me.

I started walking to the fishing spot I was going to fish under the I380 bridge, and to my surprise, that fox pup followed me to where I was going, keeping about 5 feet behind me. This was unbelievable. The fox pup lay down and stayed there, watching me fish. I finally caught a small white bass, threw it to the fox pup, it picked it up and headed back to the wood from where it came. I never saw it no more after that, but all the time this was taking place, I never let my guard down, keeping a sharp eye out for the mother gray fox, just in case she came looking for her pup.

Conclusion

As I began to write these stories, it took me back to the every place that I was fishing or on my way to a fishing spot. Those are good memories. No doubt, I had some close calls, but that's nature. I have so many stories I wanted to write about, but I chose these few. I pray you enjoyed my experiences with nature and hopefully, you will have some of your own to share.

If you decide to not tell your stories in book form, you can always share them with family and friends, but most of all, they are in YOUR heart and mind forever. That's a plus when you are around rivers and lakes watching nature.

I thank God for you who will read this book!